STOP THE BUS

NATHANIEL A. TURNER, JD, MALS

Copyright © 2016 by Nathaniel A. Turner, JD, MALS

All rights reserved. No part of this publication may be reproduced, distributed, or transmitted in any form or by any means, including photocopying, recording, or other electronic or mechanical methods, without the prior written permission of the publisher except in the case of brief quotations embodied in critical reviews and certain other noncommercial uses permitted by copyright law.

ISBN 978-0-9895879-4-5

The Raising Supaman Project

11805 North Pennsylvania

Carmel, IN 46302 www.raisingsupaman.com

Cover design by Chrystopher Burns

Prepared for publication by Naeem K. Turner-Bandele

Stop The Bus: Education Reform in 31 Days

CONTENTS

Foreword   10

DAY 1 Air Mail Fiasco   18

DAY 2 America's Epidemic   20

DAY 3 Ask The Right Question   22

DAY 4 #BlackLivesMatter   25

DAY 5 Career Ready versus College Ready   28

DAY 6 Case Managers   30

DAY 7 Childbirth Reform   32

DAY 8 Critical Thinking Anyone?!   34

DAY 9 Do No Harm   36

DAY 10 Does Anyone Own A Dictionary?   38

DAY 11 Dream Killers   40

DAY 12 Help Everyone   42

DAY 13 Hierarchy Of Needs 44

DAY 14 Measure Me! 46

DAY 15 No More Time 48

DAY 16 On The Record 50

DAY 17 Public Deception 52

DAY 18 Public Service 54

DAY 19 So Fresh and So Clean 56

DAY 20 Something To Opt In To 58

DAY 21 Student Athlete 60

DAY 22 Take A Walk 62

DAY 23 The Great Education Parody 64

DAY 24 The Hostage Negotiator 66

DAY 25 The Lonely 5 Percent 68

DAY 26 The New Buzzword 70

DAY 27 The Pope Is Here   72

DAY 28 The Rule Not The Exception   74

DAY 29 We Are All Doomed   76

DAY 30 Where Do The Children Play?   78

DAY 31 Who's On First?   80

The Author   83

FOREWORD

BANG! A student kicks my office door as they pass by in the hall. Why, I wonder after my startled response dissipates. I imagine him answering, "I hate this school."

I understand. It's dreary and needs fixing up. Some teachers yell. There are lots of rules and consequences. It probably feels like a prison. It may be better than being

home, but I can imagine him saying, "At least I get to do what I want at home."

A middle school teacher told me that it is a long, hard battle to produce a lightbulb or a-ha moment in his students. He said that most of his students come to school to be with their friends but don't see value in the academics. Our education model is set up to challenge their abilities, and most kids don't appreciate the challenge, mainly because they don't see where it's leading. There isn't anything pulling them forward. Some live in war zones in their neighborhoods. Some live in war zones in their homes. Some are raising younger siblings while their parents work two or three jobs to keep the lights on.

Where do those students get a chance to be a child, to have fun, to be silly, and to run around? Where can they learn to play and learn to dream?

I share Nate Turner's passion for transforming how we are raising and educating kids. He's an advocate for all children. This is the road on which we met. We both trained hard to be good dads and to raise our kids better than we were raised. By the time our children entered their teens, we both looked around and understood that raising our own kids is necessary but not adequate. As paying members of society, our responsibility extends beyond our own offspring.

I am honored to fight alongside Nate. He is a fierce advocate for the truth and doing what's right. I share his passion for the future. We both stay up late worrying about ways to raise the bar for parents and schools, training grounds for the leaders of the future. One of Nate's greatest features is his ability to challenge the status quo with a smile and unclenched fists. He channels his anger into action and research. In his prior book Raising Supaman and his G.P.S. (Great Parenting Strategy) program for parents, Nate has employed the concepts of backward design and reverse engineering to help parents develop their own "life template" to raise their children to reach their full potential.

I have worked in urban schools for over fifteen years as a school psychologist. I see the damage we are doing, with the best of intentions, by following the same course of action over and over again. Teachers, administrators, psychologists, and counselors all fight to keep kids on track for academic targets and graduation. We miss many opportunities every day to help students find a purpose and explore their strengths. My schools are segregated by race and class. Most of the students in my schools are African-American and come from poor families. I have a front-row seat to witness the harm that is caused by the educational resegregation of poor kids of color.

The parents who have the time and energy to advocate for their children's future pluck them out of the "broken" public school and enroll them in the "high-performing" charter school down the street. The education is still free because charter schools are funded with public dollars, but parents often have to work hard to get their child enrolled and keep them enrolled, equipping them with school uniforms and meeting the charter school's expectations for performance.

My public school is an island in a sea of charter schools. Like Indianapolis and many urban

US centers, the answer to failing schools has been a privatization effort via charter schools, entrepreneurship on the public dime. They call charter schools "high performing" but research is not showing the benefit. As well conceived as a charter school may be, most are just the brighter, shinier, better-staffed version of the same old school model. They continue to sort students using passing and failing grades, placing the blame for failure in children's brains by diagnosing learning disabilities and attention deficits. They still extinguish negative behavior and reward positive behavior, a proven method for training circus animals. We have been sorting kids into educational haves and have-nots for over 200 years.

Originally, the Industrial Age rewarded this educational model by providing high-paying, low-skill jobs in manufacturing centers like Philadelphia. One reason I am a school psychologist is that my three-generation family manufacturing business in the northern industrial area of the city had to close, bowing to pressures for cheap imports. Manufacturing jobs are no longer available for graduates of a mediocre school system. The Industrial Age is over, and the world is entering the Knowledge Age. Kids need twenty-first century skills because the Knowledge Age is hiring innovators, creators, collaborators, and communicators.

There are a million school reform efforts that fail to think outside the box. The biggest point they are missing is the student in the center. There is too much talking and not enough listening. Education needs a fresh look. Education needs transformation.

Meanwhile, in Philadelphia and Indianapolis and all over the country, while their neighbors go to charter schools, the children who continue to attend urban public schools often struggle academically, behaviorally, and require more support than the average student. They are angry, they have significant learning challenges, they need mental health treatment, and they see a bleak future. In addition, many come from families with significant challenges. Their parents are the working poor and struggle to provide the upbringing that their children require. They need help. But the surviving public schools are ill-equipped to respond to their needs, understaffed and lacking in financial resources.

This situation is untenable. It cannot last. I share the urgency reflected in this collection of letters. I feel fortunate to find a fellow agent-of-change who understands the importance of knowing where things stand before we can move forward. You can't change the future unless you know where you are starting from. Nate Turner is more than a futurist. He is a practical futurist. It would be easy to rail against the inequity in the world but Nate is a schemer. He has some grand plans about where we can go once we stop the bus. But first, we *must* stop the bus.

Robert Zeitlin *(@DrRobertZeitlin) has dedicated the last twenty years working in schools, with parents in his community, and through his private practice, to raise the bar for parents. He recently wrote* Laugh More, Yell Less: A Guide to Raising Kick-Ass Kids *(available at* bit.ly/kickasskids*) and has contributed articles to the* Good Men Project, Huffington Post, *and* Safe Kids Stories. *With his wife Betsy, Robert has* *raised two amazing teens who are busy kicking ass and taking names.*

DAY 1

AIR MAIL FIASCO

Education in Indiana is disastrous. Our educational outcomes are reminiscent of the 1930s Air Mail Fiasco. During the 1930s, airplanes carrying the mail were dropping out of the sky like students dropping out of IPS.

Back then, a pilot's inability to be properly trained jeopardized the future of commercial flight and the airline industry. Today, the inability to properly educate children puts the future of Indianapolis, and to a greater extent the US economy, in jeopardy.

Wisely, the President, tired of the embarrassment of crashing planes, enlisted the aid of citizens outside the predictable directory of experts. So in 1934, outsider Edwin Link, an Indiana native, who grew up working in his father's piano repair shop, introduced the nation to the Link Trainer—a flight simulator that trained pilots without casualties.

At this moment, Indiana, chiefly Indianapolis, should follow the model used to resolve the Air Mail Fiasco. Indiana must avail itself of creative and innovative citizens for whom thinking outside the box is more than a slogan. Indiana must collaborate with those whose passion about education has no connection to their purse or wallet.

Before suffering more casualties, Indiana would be wise to ask today's Edwin Links for help.

DAY 2
AMERICA'S EPIDEMIC

There is a silent but growing epidemic in America. Potentially, the worst outbreak in the nation's history. Extremely concerning is that those first infected are children. Shamefully, infections generally last a lifetime.

If you're around a child at any time, there's a 25 percent chance you'll come face to face with a carrier of this nationally debilitating disease. If you know four children, one of those innocent precious little people will suffer the hampering effects of the disease, an unusually difficult and unnecessarily shortened life. We're talking about a dire issue. We're talking about illiteracy.[1]

One in four children, citizens of the wealth-

---

[1] "11 Facts about Literacy in America," DoSomething.org, accessed July 11, 2016, https://www.dosomething.org/facts/11-facts-about-literacy-america.

iest nation in the world, grow up illiterate. Two-thirds of students who don't read proficiently by the end of fourth grade will be on welfare. Over 70 percent of the incarcerated are incapable of reading above the fourth grade level. And children unable to read proficiently by the close of their third grade school year are 400 percent more likely to drop out.

These are drastic times, and the health of the nation is at stake. Fortunately, there's a simple cure that doesn't require drastic measures, shots, or surgery. Parents need merely commit to playing, dancing, singing, and reading[2] with children.

---

2. "Essence Partners with Too Small to Fail, a Joint Initiative of The Clinton Foundation and Next Generation, to Promote Early Vocabulary Development Among African-American Children, Ages 0 to 5," Too Small To Fail, accessed July 11, 2016, http://toosmall.org/news/press-releases/essence-partners-with-too-small-to-fail-a-joint-initiative-of-the-clinton-foundation-

DAY 3
ASK THE RIGHT QUESTION

Pick a day, any day, and turn on the news in America. It won't be long before you see a story about the tragic death of a school-aged child. Almost immediately, the focus of the tragedy will turn to who the guilty party was and whether the child was good or bad.

Reporters, community advocates, lawyers, police officials, families, and the like all seek answers. Everyone grapples with the meaning of "justice."[3] Regrettably, when a child's life is taken, "justice" is empty. The best

---

and-next-generation-to-promote-early-vocabulary-development-among-african-american-children-ages-0-to-5.

3. Julian Grace, "Andre Green's First Run-In with IMPD Came as a Toddler," WISHTV.com, August 12, 2015, accessed July 11, 2016, http://wishtv.com/2015/08/12/andre-greens-first-run-in-with-impd-came-as-a-toddler/.

we can hope for are answers. Answers that might make it unlikely a similar tragedy will happen again.

Unfortunately, the odds are against getting the answers. We can't locate the answers because we lack the courage and integrity to ask the right questions. On the rare occasions when the answers are offered, our national state of mental illness and the hubris of our leaders block the enlightened solutions.

The tragic death of another school-aged child[4] will be repeated tomorrow and the next day and so on. Foolishly, all will do the same thing over and over again, expecting a different result.

Our nation is sick. We are insanely ill.[5]

---

4. "Family looks for answers after police kill 15-year-old," USA Today, August 14, 2015, accessed July 11, 2016, http://www.usatoday.com/videos/news/nation/2015/08/14/31699561/.
5. Michelle Healy, "Study: 20 young people a

Now ask the right question—Why?

---

day hospitalized for gun injuries," USA Today, January 27, 2014, accessed July 11, 2016, http://www.usatoday.com/story/news/nation/2014/01/27/guns-children-hospitalizations/4796999/.

DAY 4

#BLACKLIVESMATTER

#BlackLivesMatter. Is this hashtag anything more than a cute catchphrase or marketing motto? Some argue it's an affirmation of the relevance of Black people. Others argue it's a trifling annoyance—routinely associated with an unlawful civil disturbance. Still others, like me, wonder if #BlackLivesMatter is anything other than an enigma wrapped inside a contradiction.[6]

Perhaps you can answer a couple of questions that will go a long way to resolving any and all confusion about #BlackLivesMatter. First, if Black lives matter, why is it that

---

6. Katy Hall, Alissa Scheller, and Jan Diehm, "The Horrific Risk Of Gun Violence For Black Kids In America, In 4 Charts," The Huffington Post, August 19, 2014, accessed July 11, 2016, http://www.huffingtonpost.com/2014/08/19/black-children-gun-deaths_n_5692423.html.

when a murder occurs—in the community—the size and rabidness of those seeking justice is dependent not on whether there was an actual crime but on the race of the perpetrator?[7]

Second, why is it that when a police officer is the offender, the displays of anger are ubiquitous and the accompanying roar of the #BlackLivesMatter crowd reaches deafening levels? Third, why is it that when the lawbreaker is an ethnic member of the community—which is commonly the case—the #BlackLivesMatter mob is invisible and silent?[8]

---

7. Michael Daly, "How One Mother Lost Three Kids to Chiraq Over Three Decades," The Daily Beast, June 24, 2015, accessed July 11, 2016, http://www.thedailybeast.com/articles/2015/06/24/how-one-mother-lost-three-kids-to-chiraq-over-three-decades.html.

8. Dallas Franklin, "'A little girl is dead'" – Frustrated mom's #BlackLivesMatter Facebook rant goes viral," KFOR.com, August 22,

So I'll end where I started. What's the point of #BlackLivesMatter if we don't demand justice and peace for all Black lives equally?

2015, last updated August 24, 2015, accessed July 11, 2016, http://kfor.com/2015/08/22/a-little-girl-is- dead-frustrated-moms-black-livesmatter-facebook-rant-goes-viral/.

DAY 5

CAREER READY VERSUS COLLEGE READY

Would you please stop proposing career ready as an educational strategy? No matter how many times career ready is tendered, it's not a strategy. Career ready is the "My dog ate my homework" excuse, disingenuous and flawed.

Being career ready today means career extinct tomorrow. When I was a student, the same career ready advocates—who are again proposing that children forgo college readiness—suggested that poor and uninformed families aim for being ready for the careers of the day. Rather than employing a strategy where ALL students were proficient in English, mathematics, reading, and science, the career ready proponents devised a new category of child—not college material.

The not college material students attended special classes and career centers where they were trained for secure jobs such as bank tellers, cashiers, receptionists, mail carriers, newspaper reporters, librarians, travel agents, and personal assistants. In almost no time, technology had reduced or eliminated those stable careers that poor and uniformed students had been readied to work.

Career ready was not then nor will it ever be an educated solution. Preparing ALL students to be college ready is the only solution. Let's give ALL children the option to choose multiple careers whenever they are ready.

DAY 6
CASE MANAGERS

If you ask an accomplished person about their secret to success, they'll begin by explaining their process—the precise sequence of steps habitually followed to reach an intended goal. Without pausing to breathe, they'll introduce you to the person who—for lack of a better description—is their case manager.

For the accomplished, everything depends on the strict execution of the process. An exacting execution that relies on coordination. And the case manager is the person responsible for coordination.

There appears to be a rule of thumb that every time anyone is committed to a goal, they appoint someone to manage their plan of action. Well, almost every time. Except when it comes to children where the concept of a case manager has carelessly found its application typically when children are in crisis.

What if instead of waiting until a case manager was assigned by civil or criminal authorities, parents embraced their genetic appointment as case managers? What if parents cherished rather than neglected their chromosomal responsibility for controlling the process to help their children succeed?

Imagine the educational outcomes if all children had parents who followed the process for success and who admirably served as their children's case managers?

DAY 7

CHILDBIRTH REFORM

Google "school reform," and in the blink of an eye, there will be countless numbers of precise search results. Google "childbirth reform" and look closely, as none of the voluminous search results will include a specific detailed explanation for childbirth reform.

The fact that Google returns no exact search results for childbirth reform is a major reason why we have a school reform issue. Children attend school, but for some odd reason, there is no corresponding outcry to reform the process that brings children to school.

No, I'm not talking about those hideous yellow buses, either. If we are serious about improving educational outcomes universally, this is not an option. School reform begins at home—long before hormones have an opportunity to mislead the unprepared.

Transforming all schools into world-class

educational centers means equipping every parent—before the moment hits—with a foundational roadmap, basic tools, and standard techniques to help their children years before their first day of school. Without first revolutionizing the adult behavior that makes children students, school reform is pointless.

DAY 8

CRITICAL THINKING ANYONE?!

Reading your article today underscores for me the uncertainties about our nation's ability to think critically. The tone and context of your article confirm that the time is long overdue to include "journalists," along with children, in the growing list of Americans inept at critical thinking. There is just no nice way to put this; your article was asinine.

Are men so fragile that the media is required to report "Men fight back against youth violence with high-fives and cheers"?[9] Do you believe a morning of high-fives and accompanying "You're the man" exclamations

---

9. Justin L. Mack, "Men fight back against youth violence with high-fives and cheers," Indianapolis Star, October 5, 2015, accessed July 11, 2016, http://www.indystar.com/story/news/crime/2015/10/05/fighting-back-against-youth-violence-men-give-high-fives-and-cheers-middle-schoolers/73391206/.

will enable students to reach their potential? Answering either question is unnecessary.

You had the opportunity to inspire reflection and promote a measurable community action plan. You could have encouraged the community to think critically. Instead, you elected to applaud men for action which has no quantifiable educational impact—high-fives and cheers.

Hopefully, next time, you'll compel men to save their high-fives and cheers until after all students' reading and math proficiencies are increased? Perhaps in the future, you'll oblige men to reserve their high-fives and cheers until after the school achieves an average SAT score that exceeds the national benchmark.[10]

---

10. Peter VanWylen, "EdGap Map," EdGap.org, accessed July 11, 2016, http://www.edgap.org/#12/39.8113/-86.2101.

DAY 9

DO NO HARM

If you know anything about medicine, you probably have some familiarity with clinical trials. Clinical trials are a medical researcher's way of asking and answering questions about a disease and/or the treatment of the disease. As a result of clinical trials, researchers are able to determine whether medications and treatments are safe and effective for a particular condition.

The ordinary process for clinical trials is to start with a small number of subjects and progress to a larger subset only if the treatment shows potential benefits. The adherence to this crawl before you run process occurs in an effort to abide by an unwritten medical oath—First, do no harm.

You don't need a microscope to see the educational industry's sickness or to see how a similar oath would improve its condition. It doesn't matter if you name the oath the

Dewey or the Mann—just establish an oath.

Afflicted schools would recover if an oath existed compelling educators to adhere to lifesaving ethical standards. Schools could become centers for expert teaching, verified learning methodologies, and legitimate servant leadership. Then children would no longer be in the care of an educational industry that treats them like Big Pharma's[11] laboratory rats.

---

11. Andrew Pollack, "Drug Goes From $13.50 a Tablet to $750, Overnight," New York Times, September 20, 2015, accessed July 11, 2016, http://www.nytimes.com/2015/09/21/business/a-huge-overnight-increase-in-a-drugs-price-raises-protests.html?_r=3.

DAY 10

DOES ANYONE OWN A DICTIONARY?

Does anyone own a dictionary anymore? And when I ask anyone, I'm specifically questioning the growing number of organizations who keep opening schools in urban centers.

Take a moment to look at names on the school buildings. When you do, here's what you will discover. You'll find that if you assessed these schools solely by the adjectives in their names—which is unfortunately what urban parents typically do—you would believe these urban schools were the world's best. Nothing could be more untrue.

Oh, and while we are searching for a dictionary, would somebody take a moment to analyze the latest SAT and ACT results? You will find that there is little to no positive correlation between national benchmarks of college and career readiness and the hyperbolic names of most urban schools. But shouldn't there be?

So in the melodic stylings of the late Marvin Gaye, "What's going on?" Why are urban schools receiving names like Accelerated, College Prep, Elite Prep, Christian Academy, Academy for Excellence, Leadership Academy, and Preparatory Magnet?

The answer is simple. Organizations don't believe parents own dictionaries. Moreover, organizations think parents are too lazy to research terms like "false" and "deceptive advertising."

DAY 11

DREAM KILLERS

In graduate school, I took a course entitled Death and Dying. It should come as no surprise to learn that Death and Dying was about the final stage of life—dying and death.

Sadly, education reminds me a great deal of my graduate school course. So many of the schools we send children to are already dead or dying. And I'm not just talking about the brick and mortar ones, either.

Those who are honest about the walking dead status of schools are very familiar with two common contributors to schools' terminal state—incompetent creativity and illogical innovation. There is one additional, lesser known, factor contributing to the life support status of schools—dream killers.

Not only are children being set up to die a slow and painful death—denied daily the opportunity to become proficient in reading, writing, math, and science[12] —the speed of their deaths is accelerated by a unionized army of dream killers. Dead and dying educators—dreamless themselves; many of whom find great satisfaction as they sleep-walk toward retirement—have been gifted the supreme responsibility of training and inspiring tomorrow's visionaries.

Do we even need to ask why the world's greatest country ranks sixth in world innovation?[13]

---

12. Programme for International Student Assessment (Paris: Organisation for Economic Cooperation and Development, 2014) PDF.

13. Peter Coy, "The Bloomberg Innovation Index," Bloomberg.com, February 2015, accessed July 11, 2016, http://www.bloomberg.com/graphics/2015-innovative-countries/.

DAY 12

HELP EVERYONE

"Everyone needs to put some skin in the game" and "You can't help everyone" are everyday aphorisms. Despite their general truths, we must stop using trite clichés as if they were heavenly commandments for interacting with the underserved.

My guess is that neither of these trite, irresponsible sayings is new to you. I bet you've senselessly uttered them too. Privileged people have a habit of speaking without thinking. Do the world a favor, don't ever say them again!

FYI, the underserved and underrepresented have been beaten down so badly by the society we've created that they no longer have the skin to maneuver through each day let alone play a game. Families who live in abject poverty and children who suffer ACEs are like the slave who has been sadistically beaten down to the white meat. They have no skin to put in. They barely have skin at all!

And "You can't help everyone" makes sense only if you and those you love get saved. For the abandoned who wait to be saved and long for liberation, learning that someone else was protected and delivered is no consolation.

Unless those without skin tell you they don't want help, help everyone!

DAY 13

HIERARCHY OF NEEDS

In 1943, Abraham Maslow introduced his hierarchy of needs theory. According to Maslow, human beings can't evolve to our highest level of thought and behavior, self-actualization, until our physiological, safety, love/belonging, and esteem needs are met.

Maslow's theory has numerous applications, including education. Applying the hierarchy of needs theory to education infers that humans can't focus on school when they're hungry, naked, and homeless.

Pairing Maslow's transcendent research with the US economy makes it clear why our nation's educational system is appallingly deficient. In the US, 22 percent, or more than 16 million children,[14] reside in households

---

14. "Child Poverty," National Center for Children in Poverty, accessed July 11, 2016, http://www.nccp.org/topics/childpoverty.

that fall below the $23,550 federal poverty level. When calculating the cost of basic living expenses, the real percentage of impoverished children expands to an unacceptable 45 percent.[15]

How dare we expect world-class educational results knowing we've sentenced nearly half of our children to households lacking basic needs such as food, clothing, and shelter? How dare we bemoan nominal parental engagement when the majority of parents were themselves condemned a generation ago—deviously fated—incapable of satisfying their own basic needs?

If we're serious about education, it's time to develop a national conscience that considers it immoral, unacceptable, and illegal for anyone's basic needs to go unmet.

---

html.

15. "Child Poverty," National Center for Children in Poverty, accessed July 11, 2016, http://www.nccp.org/topics/childpoverty.html.

DAY 14

MEASURE ME!

There is an interesting dichotomy that exists in education—measurement. There are those who believe everything can and should be measured. And there are others who believe measurements are overrated and unnecessary.

Parents and teachers often stand on opposite sides of the measurement debate. In many districts, parents believe children are measured incorrectly and too frequently. In those same districts, teachers know that measurements are necessary and a requirement of their profession.

Although parents and teachers are often rivals when it comes to the frequency and appropriateness of measuring children, parents, and teachers manage to find common ground on one aspect of measurement. When it's time to measure either of them, both prefer not to be measured.

Parents and teachers would like to function with impunity. Generally, moms and dads believe that the word "parent" bestows some celestial power that makes them right in all childrearing matters. Similarly, educators believe the word "teacher" confers some skill doled out at birth to the exceptional few. Both are wrong; both should be measured.

Parenting and teaching are skills like reading, writing, and arithmetic. The best parents and teachers, like great students, are those who are unafraid of and embrace being measured.

DAY 15

NO MORE TIME

The other afternoon, while watching and listening to a panel of educational experts pontificate profusely about the state of education, I heard those words. One after another, each "expert" brazenly affirmed that spine-tingling expression—the declaration that would raise my hair if I wasn't already follically challenged—"It just takes time."

Who has time? The window to lay a successful academic foundation often closes by the third grade. Surely, "experts"—whose own children are reading and doing math proficiently or above grade level—weren't implying that poor and/or minority parents should continue to wait for their children's turn at world-class, high-quality education.

According to the NAEP, poor and minority children make up the bulk of fourth-grade students who failed to reach the proficient level in reading.[16] Poor and minority fourth graders perform significantly below their White and Asian classmates in mathematics proficiency.

If only the educational experts had convened at the Apollo. "Sandman" would have tap danced his way onto the stage and given each "expert" the hook. Thrown off stage—one by one—because their "More Time" act was disgraceful.[17]

"It just takes time" wouldn't play at the Apollo; it shouldn't play anywhere. Poor and/or minority families are out of time!

---

16. *Early Warning Confirmed: A Research Update on Third-Grade Reading* (Baltimore: Annie E. Casey Foundation, November 29, 2013), PDF.
17. 2013 Mathematics and Reading, The Nation's Report Card, November 2013, accessed July 11, 2016, http://www.nationsreportcard.gov/reading_math_2013/#/student-groups.

DAY 16

ON THE RECORD

Enough already! Can you please find another "national expert" or "community activist" to feature? Isn't it obvious by now that all they do is rehash the same depressing stats, quote catchy phrases, rile up an audience, point fingers conveniently and expertly at everyone but themselves, accept a handsome appearance fee, and then catch a plane to their next gig.

In case you didn't understand what you wrote, your "expert" offers no SMART process for change. Not a single word you wrote indicates your activist is capable of the breadth or depth of true contemplation.

Yet despite their mindless statements and superficial thoughts, you continue to showcase them as someone the community should know and follow. If one didn't know better, one might surmise you aren't a newspaper but rather an off-the-record advertising agency.

What's the point of the First Amendment if you aren't going to serve the people with all the facts and the whole truth? Is the First Amendment necessary when a consistent brand of people and the exact same ideas are served up to the public over and over again?

On the record, your newspaper is the reason urban communities are having such a hard time.

DAY 17
PUBLIC DECEPTION

You were there and witnessed it but chose not to report it. Another public deception disguised as a public discussion.

Yesterday's "public discussion" was like all the "public discussions" we've had in the community since schools were desegregated. Poor black and brown people are invited to the "public discussion" so that one powerful "public service" organization can tell poor black and brown people that they alone have our community's educational best interests at heart and warn us about conspiratorial, powerful, and nefarious "public service" organizations.

Since 1954, Republican–Democratic, Liberal–Conservative, For Profit–Not-For-Profit, Black and White organizations alike have all marched in to take their turn at the community podium. Yet no matter who organized the public discussion or who proclaimed their support of the community the loudest, the socioeconomic and educational status of poor black and brown people has remained virtually unchanged. Despite colorful charts and graphs and persuasive data and rhetoric, poor black and brown people continue to linger at the bottom of just about every positive social economic and educational benchmark.

Outcomes have meaning. Thus it appears that neither group—pro or anti—has ever actually helped the community.

Yesterday was another public deception, not a public discussion!

DAY 18
PUBLIC SERVICE

This can't be the first time you've heard this, yet it bears repeating—public service is not about you. At some point, someone must have mentioned that public service means you're a servant for the public. You serve the people. The people don't serve you!

Your role mandates that you serve at the pleasure of the people. Thus, you must talk with parents to know what they need and want. Your position commands you to arm parents with the facts and allow parents to make the best informed decision.

Informed parents understand the importance of school engagement. Enlightened parents will always zealously advocate for their children. Stop underestimating the power of knowledgeable parents to make schools great.

From this point forward, STOP telling parents what to do. STOP inserting your over-inflated ego into the public service equation. STOP passing laws and establishing funding priorities based on your financial interests, social relationships, and political biases.

Your public service philosophy should mirror the scripture: "Give a man a fish, you feed him for a day; teach a man to fish, you feed him for a lifetime." Patronize parents, children might improve for a moment; inform parents, children will exceed societal expectations continuously.

DAY 19

SO FRESH AND SO CLEAN

Great education is like water; it is best when it's clear and clean. Unfortunately, too many children are forced to attend schools where outcomes are cloudy and leadership is polluted.

Choose any American city and you can find a school, or worse, a school district, where misleading graduation rates, fraudulent test scores, and misappropriation of funds are the norm. In too many cities, schools are behaving so badly that if they were students, they would be expelled permanently.

Notwithstanding the obvious filth, these wayward schools are rarely closed. The "educators" are almost never banished from education. I don't believe it would be overreaching if these bad schools and horrendous "educators" were not only ousted from the practice of education but were also charged with treason.

What could be more treacherous than failing to provide all children with the skills and tools to keep the country moving forward? What could be a worse form of betrayal than to deny all children the opportunity to make a meaningful contribution to society? Is there anything more subversive than denying all citizens the right to life, liberty, and the pursuit of happiness? Don't all children deserve an education that is so fresh and so clean?

DAY 20

SOMETHING TO OPT IN TO

"Opt out," like other American movements, originated with a small well-intentioned group proclaiming a desire to serve the masses. And like other misguided efforts, what should have been a strategic planning session aimed at serving our most vulnerable citizens has instead become another American example of wasted time, resources, and energy.

Ironically, when it benefits them, the same people opposing the merits of tests are the undisputed champions for testing. The parent whose child is diagnosed with cancer pleads for the doctor who took and passed a plethora of exams. Strangely, the parent of the sick child doesn't welcome care from the doctor who opted out of the MCAT[18] and/or

---

18. "Taking the MCAT Exam," AAMC.org, accessed July 11, 2016, https://students-residents.aamc.org/applying-medical-school/taking-mcat-exam/.

the Medical Licensing Examination.

Similarly, the parent who boards an airplane to visit colleges with their child hopes and prays that the pilot has been examined and reexamined over and over again. Every passenger, including the opt out advocate, gets on the plane fully expecting that neither the pilot nor copilot was allowed to opt out of the FAA Airman Knowledge Test.[19]

To test or not to test is the wrong question. The question is will all children receive an education permitting them to opt into life, liberty, and the pursuit of happiness?

---

19. *FAA Airman Knowledge Testing Applicant Identification, Information Verification, & Authorization Requirements Matrix* (Washington, DC: Federal Aviation Administration, June 13, 2016), PDF.

DAY 21

STUDENT ATHLETE

Another Indiana school board does the unthinkable. South Bend Community School Corporation (SBCSC) dropped the academic eligibility requirements for student–athletes.[20] I'm not exaggerating when I tell you that adult common sense—similar to the US's educational ranking—has hit an all-time low.

Now to be an eligible student–athlete, one need only spell the school's name, identify the school mascot from a police-like lineup of high school mascots, and pick two crayons that are the closest match to the school's uniform colors. If a student can meet those strict scholastic standards, they are awarded the most honored student–athlete distinction.

Most student–athletes dream of playing in

---

20. Associated Press, "South Bend lowers GPA for students to play sports," Indianapolis Star, August 4, 2015, accessed July 11, 2016, http://www.indystar.com/story/news/education/2015/08/04/south-bend-lowers-gpa-students-play-sports/31101483/.

college. Yet only a select few student–athletes have a real chance of doing so. According to the NCAA, the odds of playing in college are slim, and the odds of playing professionally are almost none.[21] This irresponsible policy makes it painfully clear that the Mensas elected to serve on the school board don't appreciate the odds nor understand the NCAA eligibility requirements.[22]

FYI: The lower the GPA, the higher the required SAT or ACT score. Thanks, SBCSC, for a policy that turned slim odds into it ain't never gonna happen.

---

21. Estimated Probability of Competing in College Athletics (Indianapolis: National Collegiate Athletic Association, April 13, 2015), PDF.
22. NCAA Eligibility Center, accessed July 11, 2016, http://web3.ncaa.org/ECWR2/NCAA_EMS/NCAA.jsp.

DAY 22

TAKE A WALK

Instead of berating urban children and their parents, you should take a walk outside your ivory tower. Once you are outside, I suggest you try walking in the shoes of those you so eagerly rebuke.

It has been suggested that when you walk in another's shoes, you gain perspective. You believe urban students are unintelligent and lazy and that their parents are uncaring and absent. Your views are clear indications that you are in desperate need of perspective.

Imagine your mental acuity if you resided in a neighborhood that was absent grocery stores, safe parks, healthy restaurants, and upscale retail. Try to sense the state of your emotional health if you lived in a community where coffee shops, farmer's markets, fitness centers, and yoga studios were unavailable. Envision your spiritual well-being if every errand required a car, public transportation options were dangerous and minimal, there were no bike paths, and crime was rampant.

How focused would you be each day?
Would your disposition ever be unpleasant?
Do you think your educational outcomes might be different?

Too often, not only do people speak without thinking but we do so without any contextual experience. Do yourself a favor and take a walk.

DAY 23
THE GREAT EDUCATION PARODY

When I first received the invitation to your Great Schools events, I laughed out loud. What your organization displayed in a sentence with Great Schools was like Eddie Murphy clowning in an old SNL skit—side-splitting hilarity.

I feel terrible about laughing now. Oh, I still believe you are nothing more than a comedic spoof about great education. However, I realize your intended target audience—those families you betray daily who are desperate for great schools—view your events as real and factual.

Those hoodwinked families expecting education to deliver them from high crime and impoverished neighborhoods believe you are a PBS documentary. You and I know that you are fiction, not nonfiction. We both know your organization's cast is comprised of amateurs skilled at performing bad fiction. You are The Great Education Parody.

Your intent must be parody. For what other reason would you describe a school as great when fewer than 60 percent of the students pass the state-mandated educational exam? Your cast (staff) must be amateurs. Why else would they deliberately and purposely support depicting any education that graduates approximately 50 percent of African-American males as great?

Do the community a favor. Give nonfiction a try. Get out of comedy!

DAY 24

THE HOSTAGE NEGOTIATOR

Another school reform event…experts eight and parents zero. As in eight experts but not one parent invited to sit on the panel.

It seems unfathomable to think about school and the children who attend them without considering the parents. Yet the educational and political powers that be

seem happiest when they plot a child's future without any input from the child's parents.

Too often, parents are merely an educational afterthought. Parents are distractions—inanimate objects to be tossed aside to and fro the very same way a dog flings its chew toy. This parental disengagement approach is more than disrespectful, it's downright egregious.

The disdain shown parents is palpable. Educators treat parents as if they are terroristic hijackers who have taken the school's children hostage. But parents aren't terroristic hijackers. As parents of the children, they are community stakeholders. However, if by some stretch of the imagination, parents actually were terroristic hijackers, the educators' technique is all wrong.

Hostage negotiators create an open line of communication and are active listeners. Hostage negotiators express empathy, seeking to satisfy the hijackers' and hostages' basic needs. Hostage negotiators do something else educators don't do, they develop a rapport with the hijackers.

DAY 25

THE LONELY 5 PERCENT

New school year, same scandalous academic results soon to follow. For instance, only 5 percent of African-American high school graduates are college ready [23]. In relation to Indiana, that's 5 percent as in one, two, three, four, and five out of every hundred African-American high school graduates.

If 5 percent isn't outrageous enough, consider this: the educational, governmental, and community partners that champion education don't have a SMART plan to remedy this atrocity. Worse, rather than tell the truth to the parents of the ill-fated 95 percent, those entrusted with educating children are

---

23. Amos, Jason. "THE CONDITION OF COLLEGE & CAREER READINESS: Only 5 Percent of African American High School Graduates." Alliance For Excellent Education. March 31, 2014. Accessed September 1, 2016. http://all4ed.org/articles/the-condition-of-college-career-readiness-only-5-percent-of-african-american-high-school-graduates-college-ready-in-all-four-of-acts-college-readiness-benchmarks/.

celebrated for pathetic ISTEP scores, dishonest graduation rates, and reduced suspensions.

While ISTEP scores, graduation rates, and reduced suspensions may be mile markers on the educational journey, trifling attainments shouldn't be celebrated. Celebrations should be reserved for the day when ALL children not only graduate but do so college ready.

Anyone pursuing less than 100 percent college readiness should be rebuked and fired. And for those who find this position too harsh, answer this: Would it ever be acceptable if your car started only 5 percent of the time, if your lights came on only 5 percent of the time, or if you were able to eat only 5 percent of the time?

DAY 26

THE NEW BUZZWORD

When it comes to helping underserved and underrepresented populations, there are several customarily evoked buzzwords. One of those buzzwords is mentoring.

From the grassroots level all the way to the White House, there is a misguided belief that mentoring children is a panacea for what ails America's urban schools.

Those who endorse mentoring as an all-purpose cure-all have simply chosen to do what is familiar and easy—walk lock-step with all the others who are well intentioned but nonetheless lost. Mentoring children is not the solution for problems in urban schools.

America cannot solve the problems children face in urban schools by mentoring them away. There aren't enough qualified and dedicated mentors on the planet.

As it stands, many children are already being mentored by bighearted people who are vastly overcommitted. An unfortunate consequence of the qualified mentor shortage[24] has been

entrusting children to people who are unfit to mentor—people who have no business being in proximity to any child.[25]

If we are going to improve urban schools and communities, mothers and fathers will need to be trained to be parents. If anyone needs advice and guidance, it's the parents of the children, not the children, who need mentoring.

---

24. Anastasia Dawson, "At-risk youth face long wait for mentors at Big Brothers Big Sisters," Tampa Bay Times, May 31, 2015, accessed July 11, 2016, http://www.tbo.com/news/breaking-news/at-risk-youth-face-long-wait-for-mentors-at-big-brothers-big-sisters-20150531/.

25. Bret Lemoine, "'I Was Outraged – Disgusted:' Mentor Accused of Exposing Himself inside MPS Thurston Woods Academy," FOX-6Now.com, June 23, 2015, accessed July 11, 2016, http://fox6now.com/2015/06/23/i-was-outraged-disgusted-mentor-accused-of-exposing-himself-to-boy-inside-mpsthurston-woods-academy/.

DAY 27
THE POPE IS HERE

Instead of trivializing and monetizing the Pope's visit,[26] as some Americans will do, Pope Francis's arrival provides other citizens the perfect opportunity for self-reflection. Parents, for example, should use this historical visit as an opportunity to examine the Pope's upbringing.[27] Wise parents could go a step further and explore the pontiff's educational background.[28]

Forgive me if this sounds sacrilegious, but

---

26. Antonia Blumberg, "How Much Is Pope Francis's Visit Costing The U.S.?" The Huffington Post, September 21, 2015, accessed July 11, 2016, http://www.huffingtonpost.com/entry/pope-francis-us-visit-cost_us_56006cfbe4b0fde8b0cf693d.

27. "How Pope Francis' Upbringing Shaped His Role as Reformer," PBS NewsHour, December 25, 2014, accessed July 11, 2016, http://www.pbs.org/newshour/bb/pope-francis-upbringing-shaped-role-reformer/.

28. Seth Cline, "10 Things You Didn't Know About Pope Francis: The new pope is an avid soccer fan and has only one lung," U.S. News & World Report, March 14, 2013, accessed July 11, 2016, http://www.usnews.com/news/articles/2013/03/14/10-things-you-didnt-know-about-pope-francis.

Pope Francis is a "bad man." Not only is he the Holy Father but, more importantly, Pope Francis is someone all children can be—a Renaissance man, or woman, or as I'm almost certain he would say.

Pope Francis is a tremendously versatile, accomplished person. He is a polyglot—fluent in Spanish, Italian, and German. He has a STEM background, earning a secondary diploma in chemistry. He also holds a doctorate of theology.

Regardless of your position on religion, you must admit that Pope Francis symbolizes the type of intellectual achievement America should desire and advocate for all her children. Moreover, I'm sure you and the Pope would agree that like his long-awaited visit, America is behind schedule when it comes to graduating students and producing citizens who are knowledgeable, educated, and proficient in a multitude of subjects.

DAY 28

THE RULE NOT THE EXCEPTION

I enjoy a good rags to riches story like everyone else. Nevertheless, it seems there is entirely too much attention given to outliers. Almost every time examples of success are highlighted, the spotlight shines directly on exceptions rather than the rule.

The endorsed educational literature tells stories of overachievers and overcomers. The blockbuster movies feature the victorious transformation of underdogs and the downtrodden. Highly sought after motivational speakers recount how they turned personal tragedy into triumph.

At every turn, we show and tell children they can be the next (insert name). Despite having zip codes forcing many to attend some of the worst schools in the country, we expect all children to believe they have everything required to be an outlier. There's always a statistical probability that one socioeconomically disadvantaged student becomes the one in a million outlier who against all odds is awarded the unenviable burden of representing their entire neighborhood—but don't children deserve a better strategy than improbability?

Children need more than long odds, inspirational stories, tear-jerking movies, and motivational speeches. Children need custom-made life plans—meticulously designed with the end in mind. And America needs successful children to become the rule, not the exception.

DAY 29

WE ARE ALL DOOMED

It's little wonder why children perform so poorly academically. Parents are just not serious about school. Well, at least not enough are serious about the true purpose of education—enlightenment.

When I talk to parents about how their children are doing academically, many parents mistakenly believe we should be talking about extracurricular activities. I want to share ways to measure and improve what are most likely their son's mathematical deficiencies, but fathers prefer to share their son's tackling proficiency. I offer websites to improve literacy in large chunks, yet mothers favor celebrating their baby's popularity and how excited the crowd gets when he dunks.

Trying to help daughters offers a similarly sad opposition to reality. Excuse me, but I thought we wanted all girls to pursue the premier occupational positions and earn the highest possible salary. "Come watch my baby girl on the track, on the court, on the field…she's really good," the bulk of parents say, unaware that our parental obliviousness is setting back the progress of women in every way.

I almost hate to admit this—our children's future looks bleak. Don't wait until the new dark ages to acknowledge the truth in the words I speak.

DAY 30

WHERE DO THE CHILDREN PLAY?

Driving through my hometown this weekend was like being cast in a 1970s Cat Stevens video. Forty-five years after "Where Do the Children Play?" was released, maneuvering in and around Gary confirmed that when it comes to the children of urban public schools, Cat Stevens's question remains unanswered.

The weather was beautiful. It was sunny, and the temperature was in the low 80s. Sadly, in cities like Gary, beautiful days are not invitations to come out and play. You see, in decayed and depressed urban communities, beautiful days are the nastiest days. Beautiful days are days when children are encouraged and sometimes even forced to stay inside.

On Saturday, the children of Gary were not inside because of unseasonable temperatures or fierce storms. The children of Gary were inside—once again—because of coldhearted, senseless violence and raining bullets.[29] In the last seven days alone, there have been eight confirmed homicides.

Play matters! Play gives children the chance to blow off steam, which contributes to improved learning. Play introduces children to social rights and responsibilities, which contributes to better communities. Play is a prescription for living a longer and fuller life.

For God's sake, please let the children play.

---

29. Ben Bradley, "Gary grapples with surging murder rate," ABC7 Eyewitness News, August 4, 2015, accessed July 11, 2016, http://abc7chicago.com/news/gary-grapples-with-surging-murder-rate-/902787/.

DAY 31

WHO'S ON FIRST?

School accountability is reminiscent of Abbott and Costello's 1930s "Who's on first?" comedy routine. Discovering how and why urban schools are routinely at the bottom of positive academic measures and regularly at the top of negative social behaviors is a nonstop exercise in unresponsiveness and ambiguity.

There's no uniform answer for who's responsible for failing schools and low-performing students. There is no standardized response for how the SAT scores fell to the lowest level in the past ten years.[30] There's no homogenously transparent reason why the majority of African-American students fall short of

---

30. Nick Anderson, "SAT scores at lowest level in 10 years, fueling worries about high schools,"The Washington Post, September 3, 2015, accessed July 11, 2016, https://www.washingtonpost.com/local/education/sat-scores-at-lowest-level-in-10-years-fueling-worries-about-high-schools/2015/09/02/6b73ec66-5190-11e5-9812-92d5948a40f8_story.html.

college readiness benchmarks.[31]

When asked who's accountable, teachers retort, "Who's in the classroom?"; counselors reply, "Who's at home?"; community leaders respond, "Who's in government?"; parents counter, "Who's the principal?"; elected officials utter, "Who's in the other party?"

While this absurd game of School Accountability Pass the Buck is played, more urban schools fail, and student performance drops to obscene levels. "Who's on first?" is comedic genius when performed by Abbott and Costello. "Who's accountable?" is an American tragedy on display all over the country.

Who's accountable? We all are! And if we don't get our act together soon, the whole world will be laughing at us.

---

31. Caralee Adams, "African-American Students Found Falling Short of College-Readiness Benchmarks," Education Week, July 27, 2015, accessed July 11, 2016, http://blogs.edweek.org/edweek/college_bound/2015/07/failure_to_meet_college_readiness_twice_as_high_for_african-american_students.html.

THE AUTHOR

Nathaniel A. Turner was born and raised in Gary, Indiana. Despite graduating in the bottom quarter of his high school class from one of the worst and most impoverished school systems in the country, he went on to earn several degrees. Nate holds a bachelor's (accounting), a master's (theology and history) and a juris doctorate degree.

Nate is an entrepreneur and has operated a financial services practice since 1997. However, Nate's greatest passion is helping children realize what he rarely experienced growing up in Gary—feeling valued as a human being and knowing his life had a purpose.

Nate's counsel and advice are included on his blog *The Raising Supaman Project* and in his books *Raising Supaman* and *Stop The Bus*.

Nate encourages parents, guardians, and the community to raise children to become great world citizens, and he challenges us all to maximize our abilities to their fullest potential. Nate also speaks nationally and contributes to other nationally recognized blogs, publications, and radio programs.

Nate believes each day is another opportunity to share valuable experiences, methods, and resources with those charged with preparing the sons and daughters of our nation. Nate considers it a calling to make certain that OUR future is ready for this awesome journey called life.

<u>Connect with Nate</u>

Website: https://www.raisingsupaman.com

Twitter: @Supamans_Dad

Instagram: @Supamans_Dad

Facebook: https://www.facebook.com/RaisingSupaman

www.ingramcontent.com/pod-product-compliance
Lightning Source LLC
Chambersburg PA
CBHW030448300426
44112CB00009B/1218